Original title:
Foliage Fantasies

Copyright © 2025 Creative Arts Management OÜ
All rights reserved.

Author: Sophia Kingsley
ISBN HARDBACK: 978-1-80567-407-8
ISBN PAPERBACK: 978-1-80567-706-2

Whimsy in the Wilderness

In the forest where leaves whisper,
Squirrels dance, what a flipper!
A raccoon's hat, a toad's croak,
All join in, a merry joke.

Branches shake, a giggle spree,
As hedgehogs sip their herbal tea.
A butterfly wears polka dots,
While worms twist in silly knots.

The bushes play hide and seek,
With critters that so loudly squeak.
Fronds tickle the passing breeze,
Causing laughter among the trees.

A pine wears glasses, quite the sight,
While mushrooms glow, a party light.
Nature's quirks, a joyful play,
In this green realm, we frolic and sway.

The Allure of Arcadian Greens

In meadows bright with quirky blooms,
The daisies gossip, sharing room.
A cow with shades, looking cool,
And grasshoppers that kick in school.

Sunlight dances on toadstools wide,
While rabbits hop, their arms outstretched with pride.
A snail races 'gainst the sun,
Who knew slowpokes could be so fun?

Leaves chuckle as winds swirl around,
Silly creatures abound, unbound.
A pumpkin wears a dainty hat,
While crickets chirp a tune, how fat!

In bushes, the peacocks strut and sway,
Their colorful friends join in the play.
Nature's laughter fills the scene,
Where every leaf wears a giggle sheen.

Sprout and Sigh: Nature's Lullaby

In the garden, plants gossip, oh what a chatter,
The daisies debate if they're swaying from the shatter.
Lilies in pajamas, whispering with glee,
Wonder if the bees ever pay their fee.

A sunflower leans close, tells secrets of rain,
Claims it saw a squirrel doing a crazy gain.
While ferns shake their fronds, laughing in delight,
Over a snail's speed—what a comical sight!

The Colorful Canopy Chronicles

The leaves in the trees wear hats every spring,
Flaunting their colors as if they were bling.
A maple struts proudly, bright orange and gold,
While the oaks play poker, so brash and so bold.

In the shade, the squirrels hold a wild dance,
With acorns as maracas, they twirl and prance.
The birches roll dice, counting laughter, not loss,
As the wind joins the fun, turning leaves to gloss.

Petals in the Gloaming

At dusk the petals spill secrets so sweet,
A tulip winks at dusk, upon a soft seat.
Roses gossip loudly, sharing old tales,
Of a clumsy bee who forgot how to sail.

Violets giggle softly, their perfume in tow,
Watching the fireflies put on quite a show.
Daffodils giggle, with their heads held so high,
While a shy little bud dreams of taking to sky.

Nature's Enchanted Palette

In a vibrant garden, colors frolic and play,
Where shades of green and purple create a ballet.
A sprightly red beetle dons a tiny top hat,
Sipping dew from a leaf, oh, imagine that!

The violets plot mischief while blooms prance around,
Each petal a tale, each stem a new sound.
The sunflowers cheer as the sun bows below,
While the twilight ushers in fireflies' show.

Storyteller of the Soil

In a garden where gnomes have a chat,
They argue if flowers prefer cheese or a hat.
The daisies giggle, the roses just pout,
While worms in the dirt share a laugh and a shout.

The trees tell tales of the winds they've chased,
Of squirrels that dance and the bugs they've faced.
With roots deeply tangled in secrets unknown,
These plants are the jokers, the laughter they've sown.

The Weaving of Whispers

Leaves flutter softly like giggles in air,
As branches get tangled in playful hair.
The sun winks at petals all vibrant and bright,
While shadows play tag, oh what a delight!

In a patch of green, where the grass nearly sings,
The daisies conspiring to fashion some wings.
A breeze carries whispers of dreams in a loop,
As nature chuckles, forming a leafy troupe.

Boughs of Daydreams

Once a tree wished to dance in the sky,
But tripped on a root with a clumsy goodbye.
In a waltz with the wind, it twirled with a bounce,
As acorns created a humorous flounce.

Each branch is a laugh, and each leaf is a cheer,
While critters below share a joke that's sincere.
Together they frolic with sunbeams that slide,
In a fairy-tale forest where giggles abide.

Threads of Life and Light

With sunlight as thread, the webbing is spun,
From the glade to the grove, all is goofy fun.
In shadows, the flutterbugs plan a grand scheme,
To prank the old owl, oh, what a wild dream!

The flowers are stitching a colorful scene,
With petals and pollen, a vibrant routine.
Chortles erupt from a patchwork of hues,
As nature's own jesters share playful views.

The Poetry of Growing Things

In the garden, plants have dreams,
Talking to worms, or so it seems.
A radish claims it writes haikus,
While daisies gossip about the blues.

Roots dance underground, quite a sight,
Doing the cha-cha by moonlight.
Lettuce laughs, with a crispy shout,
"Why don't we just grow and sprout!"

A Mosaic of Sunlit Green

A patch of clovers wears a grin,
Tickling toes of those who spin.
Butterflies join in the fun,
With colors brighter than the sun.

A dandelion's wish is quite absurd,
"I'd like to fly like a little bird!"
Yet here it sits, roots dug in deep,
Dreaming of clouds while we all sleep.

The Scented Whispers of Twigs

Twigs are busy making plans,
Hatching schemes with busy hands.
"Let's play hide and seek!" they shout,
While squirrels sneer, running about.

Pine needles sing to the breeze,
"We'll tickle the noses of those with ease!"
A fragrant party under the light,
Where trees wear crowns and owls take flight.

When Nature Paints in Shades of Hope

Nature dances with a brush so bold,
Painting stories in hues untold.
A flower snickers, "I'm a work of art!"
While grasses giggle, never apart.

Mossy carpets tickle your feet,
With secrets hidden where sunlight meets.
Each leaf whispers a joke divine,
"Want to leaf today? It's just fine!"

Fluttering Through the Foliage

Squirrels in hats dance with glee,
Chasing shadows, wild and free.
Leaves giggle in the breezy air,
Whispers of nutty tales to share.

A butterfly winks, quite the show,
With polka dots in a funny row.
Trees chuckle as branches sway,
As if to tease the clouds at play.

Nature's Dreamscape

A peacock struts with a fancy tie,
Crows coordinate a sky-high fly.
Daisies wiggle, join the fun,
While crickets chirp a silly pun.

A rabbit dons oversized shoes,
Sits sipping chamomile with the blues.
Ladybugs giggle, what a sight,
Turn the garden into a delight.

The Hues of Hallowed Ground

Mushrooms laugh in polka dot coats,
While daisies gossip, sharing notes.
A sunflower does a silly jig,
Trying to dance with a playful fig.

The grass tickles reaches of the bee,
As thunderous clouds all want to see.
Each hue brightens the comical scene,
While butterflies plot a prank so keen.

Vines that Embrace the Sky

Twisting and turning, the vines have fun,
Wrapping around like a big, warm bun.
They giggle and whisper, "Look at me!"
As they coil round a tall pine tree.

A beanstalk starts a game of tag,
While bees zoom by with a happy brag.
The flowers laugh, oh what a scene,
Nature's antics, so silly and green.

The Gilded Canopy

Beneath the leaves, a squirrel's dance,
He wears a crown, oh what a chance!
The acorns roll like bowling balls,
As laughter echoes through the halls.

A bird in shades of gaudy hues,
Practicing its best 'superstar' views.
With every flap, it strikes a pose,
Who knew trees had such funny shows?

Silhouettes of Nature's Dreams

In shadows cast by branches wide,
A rabbit hops, it can't decide.
Should it go left or might it go right?
In the dark, it takes flight!

A raccoon with a pie, oh what glee!
He'll take a slice, but not for free.
But when the forest bursts with cheer,
You might just find a fox with beer!

Labyrinth of Leaf and Light

In a maze where sunlight plays,
A chipmunk counts its nuts for days.
Mistaken for a golden prize,
It jumps and twirls beneath the skies.

A butterfly, in search of snacks,
Keeps getting stuck on silly tracks.
It flutters, flips, an airy tease,
While ants march past with absolute ease!

Cradle of the Forest Spirits

In swaying trees, old spirits wake,
While fairies giggle, jokes they make.
With playful pranks and smiles so wide,
They dance around, the woods their slide.

A gnome, with glasses, bright and round,
Tells tall tales of the laughter found.
But when the sun begins to drop,
He trips on roots and makes a plop!

Portraits of the Painted Woods

In the depths of the trees, colors collide,
A squirrel in a bow tie, with nothing to hide.
Leaves whisper secrets, giggles take flight,
As branches dance wildly under the moonlight.

A raccoon in glasses, sips tea with a smile,
Critters recount tales that stretch for a mile.
They plot tiny pranks, oh what a delight,
While shadows play tag, ducking out of sight.

Rhythms of Resilient Roots

Roots twist and turn, like tangled old yarn,
An underground party, where no one's outworn.
Earthworms are DJs, spinning the tunes,
While gophers keep grooving beneath the full moons.

Their dance floor is muddy, but none seem to care,
A worm winks at a mole, who spins with a flair.
The rhythm of laughter rises and descends,
In this underground rave, even silence pretends.

Echoes in the Evergreen

Among the green needles, a parrot sings loud,
 He's the king of the forest, oh so avowed.
 Pinecones are records, spinning their tales,
As pine needles shimmer like fairy-tale trails.

The shadows resemble some off-beat clowns,
 Jumper on trunks, the forest compounds.
A woodpecker's drumming lights up the scene,
As echoes of laughter slide 'neath the evergreen.

The Lure of Leafy Glades

In a glade full of leaves, laughter erupts,
As chipmunks juggle acorns, how they disrupt!
A tale spins of mischief, a dash here, a twirl,
While butterflies giggle, caught in the whirl.

Underneath the bright canopies, shadows play tricks,
With a dance of confusion, they all do the mix.
The jests are contagious, you can't help but grin,
Among leafy court jesters, let the fun begin!

Meanderings Through the Underbrush

In the wild, a squirrel dances,
Chasing shadows, lost in prances.
Leaves giggle as they flutter down,
While ants parade, a tiny crown.

A rabbit wears a silly hat,
Fashioned from a fallen sprat.
Nature's jesters roam with style,
In a woodland that makes you smile.

Beneath a bush, a hedgehog sighs,
Dreaming of disco in the skies.
Frogs croak their favorite tune,
While the moon joins in, a bright balloon.

So wander through the leafy maze,
Where laughter echoes in funny ways.
Each step you take, a chuckle found,
In the underbrush, joy knows no bound.

The Flicker of Green Through the Thicket

A firefly in a top hat gleams,
Hosting parties, or so it seems.
With a twinkle, it invites the crowd,
To join in dance, lively and loud.

Beneath a bush, a lizard slides,
Wearing sunglasses, oh what pride!
With a flick of his tail, he takes a twirl,
Making all the ladybugs whirl.

The daisies gossip, petals aflutter,
Whispering secrets, sharing a nutter.
A butterfly joins with wings so bold,
As mushrooms giggle, their tales unfold.

Oh, wander on through this patchy scene,
Where the grass wears a crown of green.
In the thicket, mischief is spry,
Under the watch of a friendly sky.

Tales of Windswept Whispers

The wind tells tales of leaf and breeze,
Of funny critters with unmatched ease.
A crow in spectacles, wise and grand,
Sips from puddles, life unplanned.

A gust rustles through the lofty highs,
Chasing shadows beneath the wise.
A raccoon laughs while stealing a snack,
Dance of nature, no fear of the flack.

Bubbling brook sings a merry song,
As frogs join in, hopping along.
The whispers of leaves, they chuckle bright,
In this land where giggles take flight.

So stroll through whispers, winds so light,
In a world where humor takes flight.
With each rustle, a joke unfolds,
In the nature's realm, fun never molds.

Beneath the Bough of Dreams

Beneath a bough, a dream takes root,
A snail wears slippers, so very cute.
He slides along with such finesse,
While flowers giggle, their petals a mess.

A hedgehog spins like a top on grass,
With clover confetti, a dazzling pass.
He rolls in leaves, feeling quite spry,
As the wind gives him a gentle high-five.

Platforms of bark, where squirrels will leap,
Chasing each other with giggles so deep.
They hide in knots, play hide and seek,
Nature's playground, where fun's never bleak.

So linger long beneath these dreams,
Where laughter flows like sunny streams.
In this haven, where wonders gleam,
Life's a joke, just think, it's a dream.

Nurtured by Nectar

In the garden, bees do dance,
Sipping sweetness, what a chance!
Flowers giggle, bloom with cheer,
"Drink up, darling, lend me your ear!"

Ants parade in lines so straight,
With tiny hats, they celebrate.
"Is this a party?" one ant shouts,
"Oh yes! But watch out for the sprouts!"

Lullabies of Leafy Lull

Breezes hum a leafy tune,
Underneath the watchful moon.
Squirrels sing and jump with glee,
"Who needs sleep? Come dance with me!"

Snails in pajamas slide on by,
"Care for a race?" they slyly cry.
With slow-motion, they all trot,
In this garden, time's forgot.

The Allure of the Verdant Vale

In the vale where mushrooms dance,
Pixies twirl in floral pants.
"Join the fun!" they cheerfully tease,
"Just mind the bugs and bumblebees!"

Caterpillars wear disguises fine,
Sipping dew from a sipping vine.
"Transform to flutter!" they squeal with joy,
To be a moth, not just a boy.

Creatures of Folklore Among the Leaves

Mice in cloaks tell tales so grand,
While rabbits mix up magic sand.
"Bet you two carrots I can fly!"
With a hop and a wink, they try.

A hedgehog riddles in his shell,
"Did you hear the tale I tell?
Of feasts with crumbs and moonlit streams,
It's all much sweeter than it seems!"

The Brush of Nature's Palette

In colors bright, the leaves do dance,
With one leaf's wink, we take a chance.
A yellow hat atop a tree,
Who knew trees could be so free?

A red leaf shouts a silly joke,
While squirrels giggle, weaving smoke.
A green tree sings a funny tune,
As clouds chuckle 'neath the moon.

Breezes tease with whispers loud,
While acorns wear their hats so proud.
The branches sway, they do a jig,
Making nature's antics big!

When autumn calls, the trees all play,
A dress-up party on display.
With every rustle, laughter's near,
The woods are filled with jolly cheer!

Shadows on the Forest Floor

The shadows stretch and yawn at noon,
As rabbits mock the passing moon.
A shadow gets a bit too bold,
And trips on roots beneath the gold.

The toadstools giggle, swaying still,
As butterflies chase dreams at will.
Invisible pranks, a sneaky breeze,
Tickles the toes of ancient trees.

A fox pretends a grand vaudeville,
With every flip, it seeks a thrill.
The sunbeams laugh, they beam so bright,
Creating spots for a playful fight.

Beneath the leaves, the shadows play,
Spilling secrets in a funny way.
Majestic trunks, in jests, they soar,
In this whimsical forest lore!

Undercurrents of Verdure

Beneath the ferns, a secret plot,
Where snails are kings and jokes are hot.
A dandelion dons a crown,
As flowers giggle, painted brown.

A whispering breeze incites a laugh,
While twigs engage in a staff path.
The underbrush sways with delight,
In this leafy realm, all feels right.

A caterpillar claims its fame,
While bees enact their buzzing game.
The mossy floor, a cushy stage,
Where critters share their humor page.

With every swirl, the green does tease,
As autumn's breath stirs up the trees.
A leafy ball, they sway and play,
In the dance of nature, come what may!

Songs of the Sycamore

The sycamore sings a quirky song,
Where every note feels right or wrong.
Its branches wave like arms of cheer,
   Inviting all the critters near.

A family of squirrels joins the band,
With acorns clapping in their hands.
The crows join in with cawing notes,
While frogs croak loud in silly coats.

The melody drifts through the sun,
   A chorus that sets hearts to run.
With rustles and chuckles all around,
Nature's laughter is profoundly found.

As breezes carry the joyous tune,
The sycamore bends, under the moon.
In this whimsical harmony's call,
   The woods provide laughter for all!

Mystique of Mossy Groves

In a grove where moss wears shoes,
'Tis a dance of leaves and forest blues.
Squirrels debate in hushed, sly tones,
While rabbits hop on mossy thrones.

A turtle struts with elegant flair,
Declaring, "I'm speedy—if you dare!"
The mushrooms giggle, all in a row,
While crickets play the banjo low.

A hedgehog juggles acorns on a bet,
Only to drop them—oh, what a fret!
The trees giggle and sway with glee,
As nature laughs at the sight, you see?

So swing and sway in this grove so bright,
Where every creature has pure delight.
The mossy carpets roll out their charms,
Inviting all to dance in their arms.

Beneath the Boughs of Imagination

Under boughs, where dreams convene,
A raccoon wears a hat—quite the scene!
He sips on dew from a bamboo cup,
While a sleepy owl says, "Wake up!"

The butterflies wear polka-dot gowns,
While fireflies twirl in their tiny crowns.
They host a ball where the acorns bounce,
And chipmunks lead the dance, they pounce!

A snail slides in with an emerald tie,
Claiming he's fast—and oh, my, oh my!
The leaves are confetti as nature claps,
For beneath the boughs, nothing but laughs!

So join this fest, let worries take flight,
Where silliness reigns from day into night.
In this realm of whimsy, bright and grand,
Imagination grows in every hand.

Where Nature Weaves its Whimsy

In a patch where the wildflowers giggle,
A fox shares riddles that make you wiggle.
The daisies laugh at the tales he spins,
While the breeze hums soft, inviting grins.

The trees wear glasses, all askew,
Reading stories no one knew.
A badger critiques the fashion show,
While ladybugs strut in a flashy row!

A frog in a bowtie leaps with style,
Challenging birds to a rhythmic mile.
The grasshoppers croon in tuneful cheer,
Amidst the laughter, there's nothing to fear!

So wander here where the sunbeams play,
In this land of whimsy, joy leads the way.
With every chuckle and giggle around,
Nature spins magic, laughter abounds.

A Treetop Serenade

Up above where the branches twirl,
A raccoon sings to a dancing squirrel.
With harmonies sweet, they steal the show,
While the stars nodding, twinkle below.

The vines are swing sets for the brave,
Where laughing winds play, and the leaves wave.
A parrot critiques each note and tune,
As crickets create a night's festoon.

An owl croons softly, wise and bright,
Telling tales to the moonlight.
The fireflies blink in rhythmic beats,
As creatures gather, tapping their feet.

So join this night, oh, take a peek,
In treetops high, there's joy to seek.
With every note, the night comes alive,
In this serenade, laughter will thrive.

Whirling Wisteria Wishes

In a swirl of purple dreams,
Wisteria dances with the breeze.
A squirrel steals a berry treat,
While a bee buzzes, filled with glee.

Twisting vines and giggly greens,
Tickle the toes of passing cats.
If only trees could tell their tales,
Of secret gnomes and funny bats.

Laughter floats on fragrant air,
As petals fall like laughter's chime.
The hedgehog wears a tiny hat,
Claiming he's the king at rhyme.

So if you hear a rustling sound,
It might just be a jester's joke.
With leaves as curtains, nature's stage,
Where even sunflowers can poke!

Leafy Labyrinth

Hidden paths of green delight,
Where chubby rabbits hop with flair.
Each turn unveils a leafy joke,
Or a snail who's lost his way there.

If you seek the right vine maze,
Don't trust your nose to guide you true.
The mushrooms giggle, twinkling caps,
While squirrels play peek-a-boo!

A hasty hare thinks he's so sly,
But the mushrooms point with delight.
"Down that path! Or maybe this?"
"Oops, wrong way! Come join the flight!"

In this green circus of delight,
Laughter echoes through the leaves.
Find the exit or lose your way,
In nature's show, where nothing grieves!

The Secret Garden's Lament

In a garden where secrets bloom,
A tomato wore a fancy coat.
He struck a pose, feeling grand,
While a cantaloupe hums a note.

Nosey daisies whisper low,
"What's that over there, in the shade?"
A broccoli, with dreams of flight,
Wants to be a leafy brigade.

Rabbits gossip in moonlit spots,
Sharing tales of stolen greens.
Meanwhile, roses, beautifully bold,
Debate whether they'd like to be seen.

In a place where veggies quip,
And flowers chuckle with delight,
The garden sighs, then bursts with joy,
A hide-and-seek in soft moonlight!

Colors of the Canopy

Oh, what a riot of hues above!
Rainbow leaves dance upon the sky.
A purple tree wears a funny grin,
While the orange ones argue, oh my!

Flashing reds and yellows bright,
Chasing clouds, they play tag high.
With every gust, they twirl and spin,
Like kids on swings, who can't quite fly.

A bird dressed in flamboyant flair,
Jokes with squirrels, laughs full and bright.
"What color am I today, my friends?"
"Surprise! You're left with all the light!"

Each branch a stage, each leaf a cheer,
In the kaleidoscope's embrace.
Giggles echo through the grove,
Losing tracks in nature's race!

Tapestry of Autumn's Embrace

Leaves in sweaters, bright and bold,
   Whisper secrets of tales untold.
  Squirrels giggle, dancing round,
    In nutty laughter, joy is found.

  Pumpkin hats on every head,
Wobbling woods; the trees are wed.
  Nature's carnival, wild and free,
Boisterous creatures sing with glee.

Crimson carpets, a slippery race,
 Falling leaves in a playful chase.
  Jumpy critters make a fuss,
  As they tumble, oh what a rush!

   In this patchwork of delight,
  Nature's pranksters take to flight.
With every rustle, giggle and cheer,
The season's laughter rings so clear.

Secrets Under the Sylvan Canopy

Beneath the branches, secrets hide,
Giggling gnomes take a wild ride.
Acorns tumble, and twigs snap,
   Nature whispers a funny clap.

Dancing shadows play tag with light,
The owls wear spectacles, what a sight!
Bumblebees buzzing, a chaotic choir,
   Joking with flowers that never tire.

Silly squirrels in feathered hats,
Playing tricks on the sleeping bats.
With every breeze, a chuckle slips,
   As they waggle in flashiest clips.

Under canopies, laughter weaves,
As the breeze teases the autumn leaves.
Secrets shared, while raccoons prance,
   Under the trees, they start to dance.

Lush Reveries Beneath the Boughs

In leafy lanes where laughter blooms,
Where bugs play marbles in mushroom rooms.
Frogs on lily pads, hats askew,
Croaking jokes that tickle too.

With every rustle, a snicker grows,
Beneath the boughs where mischief flows.
Toadstools giggle, they cannot stop,
As shadows twirl and tree trunks hop.

Pixies plotting in a leafy nook,
Spinning stories as old as a book.
Wiggly worms with cheeky grins,
Join the fun as the laughter spins.

Branches bobbing in merry jest,
Nature's comedy is at its best.
Underneath this leafy dome,
The forest sings, "This is our home!"

The Green Songbird's Tale

A songbird perched with a cheeky glare,
Sings to the wind, without a care.
Wiggly worms dance in delight,
Held captive by music, oh what a sight!

He croons of sunshine, footloose and free,
Tripling tunes from his leafy tree.
Chirping laughter, a playful sound,
As the critters gather all around.

A mischief-maker with plucky style,
The bird spreads joy, singing all the while.
With a wink and a flap, he starts to sway,
Skipping through branches, come what may.

In the melody of green and cheer,
Every note brings the forest near.
With every trill and every tale,
The songbird knows, he will prevail.

The Leafy Labyrinth

In a maze where leaves play hide and seek,
A squirrel with a map thought he was unique.
He spun in circles, lost and confused,
While branches above simply laughed and amused.

A daring hare dashed with some flair,
Jogging through the ferns, full of hair.
He tripped on a twig and landed with grace,
The blossoms erupted, doubling in face.

A cactus tried dancing, or so he thought,
But with stiff little arms, he just looked distraught.
The whispers of ivy giggled in mirth,
As the cactus declared this was his rebirth.

Beneath the bright moon, the creatures all roared,
Planets of leaves tackled and soared.
In this leafy labyrinth of the absurd,
Even the wind got the last word.

Symphony of Swaying Stems

A concert of stems held an uproarious show,
Where daisies sang loud and sunflowers would glow.
The breeze played the strings while the crickets did hum,
Each petal a note, a delightful little drum.

A dapper old fern wore his finest green coat,
While snails in tuxedos wobbled to float.
They moved to the beat, so shiny and slick,
But tripped on each other—oh, what a schtick!

The clovers all danced, performing a jig,
Glittering dewdrops, they twirled like a twig.
As the moonlight shimmered, the trees clapped in time,
Nature declared, "Ladies and gents, it's sublime!"

But soon the cicadas lost track of the beat,
And all got in line for a comical seat.
As the symphony swayed, each crumb fell from trees,
An encore was planned, as they giggled with glee.

Echoes of the Forest Floor

In the underbrush, the mushrooms form queues,
Hoping for spotlight and some forest news.
A hedgehog with style hosted a grand bash,
But stumbled on acorns, causing a crash.

The bugs all convened, sporting tiny hats,
They waltzed with the beetles, the funky diplomats.
A butterfly drifted through costumes absurd,
Whispering to daisies, "I'll not be deterred!"

The shadows grew thicker, the owls took their stand,
As laughter erupted from each leafy band.
With a wink and a nod, every root did implore,
Echoes of hilarity rang from the floor.

Yet just as the night reached its funny peak,
A quiet detour left everyone meek.
For the squirrels arrived with their prize acorn stash,
And the giggles turned to roars with each comical crash.

Verdant Visions at Dusk

As dusk painted skies in delightful shades,
The plants all conspired in playful charades.
A cactus declared, "I'll paint the air pink!"
While a worm wiggled past, too shocked to think.

"Let's form a parade!" cried an enthusiastic vine,
As leaves swished and twirled, in a conga line.
The frogs cranked the tunes with a ribbit and roar,
While fireflies blinked in a show-stopping score.

Then came the hedgehogs, slipping and sliding,
With spiky little dance moves, they started gliding.
They spun round the petals, a brief breath away,
And the flowers all giggled, "What a fanciful display!"

But laughter quick faded when dawn's light broke through,
As each little creature hid from the view.
In the verdant ambiance of dreams gone amiss,
It was nothing but folly, and too funny to miss.

A Serenade Among Green Silks

In a garden where giggles grow,
Lettuce whispers, 'What do you know?'
Carrots dance in their little shoes,
While the radishes sing the blues.

Sunflowers sway to a silly tune,
Tickled by the light of the moon.
Worms put on their wiggle show,
While daisies don their best glow.

Butterflies wear their finest threads,
As grasshoppers hop on tiny beds.
An orchestra of frogs takes their place,
In the concert of leafy lace.

A breeze stirs up a cheerful jest,
Nature's heart is brightly dressed.
In green silks, laughter springs,
Every petal holds the joy it brings.

Unfolding Petals of Possibility

A dandelion dreams of being a kite,
With seeds that sail and catch the light.
Tulips giggle in their brilliant hues,
While violets share the latest news.

Petals dance in a delightful spree,
Labelling every leaf with glee.
A daisy tells tales of days gone by,
While bees buzz a humorous high.

The sun's a joker with rays that tease,
Sending warmth like a sunlit sneeze.
In this garden of playful blooms,
Every turn holds laughter's blooms.

So let's petal-paddle this joyful ride,
With a giggle at nature's side.
Unfolding dreams in colors bright,
A world of fun in pure delight.

Chronicles of the Canopy

Up in the trees, where squirrels debate,
Jokes about acorns, they simply can't wait.
A branch has claimed a throne of delight,
Where laughter rings out through day and night.

Owls wear glasses to read the stars,
And giggle over Venus's silly cars.
They ponder if clouds like to play hide,
Or if shadows just want to glide.

The wind writes stories in rustling leaves,
Whispering secrets to the hapless bees.
Bark-scribblers pen their tales with glee,
In the royal court of the old oak tree.

All is jolly in leafy courts,
As nature's jesters make their reports.
Chronicles unfold with a raucous cheer,
In the canopy where laughter's near.

Between the Branches of Belief

In the woods where giggles twist,
Trees high five, they can't resist.
Mushrooms gossip like old pals,
While acorns plot their leafy jalls.

A squirrel writes a book of tricks,
Pondering on the best nut picks.
The shadows dance in a merry swirl,
While fireflies host a light-up whirl.

Between the branches, a tale unfolds,
Of the daffodils and brave marigolds.
They sing of adventures, wild and grand,
In a whimsical, enchanted land.

With every breeze, a new tale springs,
Of laughter shared and joyful things.
So join the frolic, don't miss the show,
Between the branches where dreams do grow.

A Tangle of Tales Unraveled

In the woods where squirrels dance,
A tree once wore a fancy pants.
He twirled around with such a flair,
But lost them in the bramble's snare.

The raccoons snickered, oh what fun,
As branches whispered, 'Well, he's done!'
They hosted tea beneath the shade,
With leaves as cups, a leafy parade.

The owl hooted, wise and grand,
Said, 'Fashion's tricky in this land!'
Yet as they laughed, the trees joined in,
Their roots all wiggled, a leafy grin.

Now every morn, those critters meet,
To tell tall tales and share a treat.
In nature's laughter, life unfolds,
A story woven, bright and bold.

Green Guardians of the Grove

Beneath the shade of leafy crowns,
The guardians wear their leafy gowns.
They rustle secrets, oh so sly,
Tickling branches that wave goodbye.

The ferns all gossip, soft and low,
While daisies gossip 'bout the show.
With whispers sweet, they haul their tales,
Of fuzzy bees and sprightly snails.

The chipmunks chuckle, quick on feet,
As they hop around, a silly treat.
With acorns hats and tiny flags,
They march in time, while grass blade drags.

So if you wander where they play,
Expect a laugh or two, I say!
For in the grove, with joy they gleam,
A greener world, a giggling dream.

The Charm of the Canopied Path

On a winding path where shadows bask,
A squirrel held a question: 'What's the task?'
The trees leaned in with open arms,
Their barky laughter, full of charms.

A turtle strolled with swagger bold,
In shades of green, his story's told.
He wore a leaf, his crown so grand,
While flowers giggled at his stand.

The sunbeam peeked through branches wide,
To find a rabbit trying to hide.
With silly puns, they shared delight,
In dappled light, a funny sight.

So journey down this jolly way,
Where nature thrives in cheerful play.
With every step, the joy will sprout,
From canopies that laugh and shout.

Enigma in the Evergreens

Amongst the pines, a mystery brews,
With whispers soft of coffee snooze.
A hedgehog slept with hat askew,
While robins plotted the funny view.

They gathered tales of mischief's ride,
Of twinkling stars and breezy slide.
The branches swayed with tales untold,
Through giggles shared, their hearts consoled.

The chattering squirrels twirled about,
With nuts for treats, they jumped and spouted.
They skipped along, in playful jest,
Among the trees, they felt the best.

So when you find the secret way,
Join in the dance, come laugh and play.
For in the evergreens, joy's the key,
Unlock the fun, let laughter be!

Whispers of Leaf and Light

Rustling leaves chat with the breeze,
Tickling the branches, doing as they please.
Squirrels throw parties up high in the trees,
While ants plan their picnics, oh what a tease!

Dancing shadows play hide and seek,
A hop, skip, and jump - who's next in this peek?
Bouncing off bark, it's a game quite unique,
As saplings join in, it's a joyfully cheek!

Laughter erupts as a bird drops a nut,
It bounces and rolls with a thud and a grunt.
A worm yells, "Hey! That's a terrible stunt!"
While mushrooms all giggle, sending in their front!

In the end, the leaves whisper and chuckle,
As nature's own stories begin to sparkle.
Every twig bent under the joy's little buckle,
Leaves grinning wide, no sign of a muckle!

Canopy Dreams in Emerald

Up in the treetops, where dreams take a leap,
Squirrels wear hats, it's quite the big peep!
The owls hoot loudly, their wisdom quite deep,
While dandelion wishes float down in a sweep.

Butterflies gossip, flap-flap, flap-flap,
A ladybug winks, setting up for a nap.
Grasshoppers dance in a chittering clap,
While fireflies shimmer, making light in a map!

The shadows grow longer, it's time to convene,
A council of critters, what could they mean?
With acorns as armor, they splotch the old green,
Crafting grand tales where no one's been seen.

Whispers abound in this leafy domain,
As laughter erupts with an odd kind of strain.
Ants in their suits marching down the lane,
Each step quite the shuffle - oh, isn't it plain!

Chronicles of the Verdant Veil

In the shadows of green, a secret unfolds,
A vine-tangling story that never gets old.
With mushrooms in jackets, and frogs being bold,
They sip on sweet nectar, oh man, it's gold!

The trees boast of wisdom, gnarled and twisted,
While ivy creeps closer, a prank most unlisted.
Dancing in circles, the flora gets wristed,
It's a sidewalk sale where fun's not a miss-ted!

Laughter rings out from the bushes nearby,
As daisies wear glasses, unimpressed by the sky.
A caterpillar comments, with a wink in his eye,
"Who needs a cocoon? I prefer to slide by!"

Breezes bring whispers, a chuckle or two,
As leaves shake their heads at the nonsense they knew.
In this leafy parley, the old becomes new,
Every root and petal sings a joyful hue!

Dance of the Mossy Shadows

In mossy green corners where shadows all dance,
There's a party of critters, each croaking their chance.
To twirl with the ferns in a leafy romance,
As puffballs drift gently in a wobbly prance.

The toads wear their crowns made of glimmering dew,
And mushrooms toss confetti as critters fly through.
A festival rises, oh what a hullabaloo,
While snails slide on in, with a shimmering view!

A breeze teases petals, a flirty delight,
The daisies throw petals, from left and to right.
The trees roll their "eyes," when things get too bright,
As shadows grow longer, and day turns to night.

With giggles and whispers, the forest implores,
"Join in on the fun, there's laughter galore!"
The leaves sway in rhythm, opening new doors,
In this mossy-sweet dance, we'll always want more!

The Sway of Sylvan Dreams

In a forest of giggles, trees like to dance,
They sway with the wind, giving leaves a chance.
A squirrel in a top hat struts with great flair,
While mushrooms, they chuckle, without a care.

The sun plays peek-a-boo, what a cheeky delight,
As shadows grow longer, they fizz in twilight.
A rabbit with glasses reads jokes from a book,
While fireflies twinkle, in a sparkling nook.

A leaf on a branch makes a silly face,
Throwing down laughter in this bright, leafy place.
With whispers of laughter from vines overhead,
The trees tell tall tales, while giggling in bed.

Each breeze carries chuckles, each rustle a tease,
In this merry woods, there's always a breeze.
So come join the fun, where the wild seems absurd,
For in sylvan sweet dreams, joy's never deterred.

Above the Ferns and Feathers

Above the ferns, a parrot sings,
In a voice like a trumpet, it shares funny things.
A snail with a monocle glides on by,
While owls roll their eyes, oh my, oh my.

Tiny fronds like dancers spin with delight,
But often they trip, what a silly sight!
A pigeon pretends to be a runway star,
Wobbling and bobbling, not going far.

The feathers above tickle branches with glee,
As a chubby raccoon tries to climb a tall tree.
With giggles and squirms, they tumble and fall,
While daisies erupt in laughter, one and all.

So dance in the dirt and wobble with cheer,
In this funny old world, nothing is drear.
For above the ferns, where laughter thrives best,
Nature's a clown, putting humor to the test.

The Essence of Elusive Leaves

Leaves of green giggle beneath the blue sky,
Hiding secrets of squirrels that prance and fly.
A leaf with a grin spills tea on the ground,
While bugs tell tall tales, together they're found.

The whispers of branches, a comic affair,
A fruit bat's ballet brings gasps from the air.
With every leaf flutter, a chuckle entwines,
In this quirky world, even sunlight declines.

A gnome on a mushroom play jester, you see,
Tickling toes of a nearby wee bee.
As shadows don glasses and elbow each other,
The sun starts to giggle, "Oh brother! Oh brother!"

Each day brings a riddle wrapped up in a leaf,
Where laughter is bold, and none know of grief.
So come, take a stroll through this cheery green maze,
Where the essence of joy blooms, in whimsical ways.

Tangles of the Unseen

In tangled jungles, where mischief abounds,
The critters host parties without any bounds.
A lizard in shades slinks by, oh so sly,
While vines get all tangled, they giggle and sigh.

Behind every bush, a raccoon's throwing darts,
While squirrels are crafting odd geometrical arts.
They bust out in laughter, no care for the scene,
For humor's the heart of these tangles unseen.

Caterpillars chuckle while munching on greens,
Not knowing their future in butterfly dreams.
A leaf's clever wink as it flutters away,
Teases the branches at the end of the day.

In shadows so silly, where laughter takes flight,
The forests remind us that joy's a pure sight.
So dance through the brambles, let whimsy be free,
In this playful domain, nature's spirit we see.

Lush Tapestry of Time

In a forest where socks seem to wander,
Trees wear green hats, oh what a blunder!
The squirrels hold meetings, plotting their heist,
While the sun joins the fun, oh, isn't it nice?

Whispers of leaves in the soft morning light,
They gossip and giggle, what a delightful sight!
A bird with a tie is stuck in a tree,
Singing odd ballads, just let him be!

The shadows compete with the sun's playful quest,
Dancing like partners at a wobbly fest.
With each twirl and whirl, the grass joins the spree,
Laughing and teasing, totally carefree.

As the day wraps itself in a leafy embrace,
The creatures conspire to fill up the space.
They plan a wild party with snacks galore,
But don't serve the mushrooms! They're friends, not a score!

Petals in a Painted Breeze

In a garden of giggles where daisies do dance,
Tulips wear shoes, trying to prance.
Butterflies chuckle, their colors a riot,
"Oh look at the sunflowers, they think they're quiet!"

The bees wear sunglasses, a sight to behold,
"Life's too short!" they buzz, feeling bold.
The roses call out, "We're royal and grand!"
While the timid little violets giggle and stand.

A shadow flies over; it's just a big bird,
Dropping odd seeds, oh, haven't you heard?
The flowers all wonder, "Will we grow tall?"
But instead they just wilt, striking goofy sprawl.

As petals flamboyantly flutter about,
The humor's contagious, there's no room for doubt.
In this botanical joke, all are prime,
Where laughter's the nectar, sweet as a rhyme!

Embrace of the Emerald

In a forest of green, with mischief afoot,
A gnome has misplaced his very own boot!
"Who could be naughty?" he wonders aloud,
As the toadstools giggle, all huddled and proud.

The ferns wear grand hats, quite stylish and neat,
While the moss throws a party for those who'd dare seat.
The rabbits are rapping, a beat they create,
Bouncing and laughing, they just can't be late.

The trees whisper secrets, their bark full of jest,
Telling tales of a hedgehog who dreams of the zest.
"Let's dance in circles," they sing with delight,
While the fireflies flash like they're taking a flight.

In this realm of green, where whimsy's the rule,
Life's a hilarity — oh, what a cool duel!
As dusk drapes her cloak, the fun doesn't stop,
With dreams full of giggles, they hop and they bop!

Shimmering Underbrush

In the underbrush shimmering with playful flair,
A hedgehog in sunglasses claims he's a bear!
The snails share secrets, moving ever so slight,
While the shadows behind them are trying to bite.

The critters are gathering for their wild debut,
With bad dance moves, they don't have a clue.
The frogs leap around, croaking songs out of tune,
While the thistles critique — oh, what a cartoon!

A firefly DJ spins tracks in the glades,
While the brambles all wiggle, pulling off charades.
They laugh at the chaos, not caring a lick,
As the moon chuckles on — oh, it's quite the trick!

So here in the shadows where fun takes its place,
With laughter and mischief, they spin in the space.
In this glowing underbrush, joy's the decree,
Where the night's just a party for you and for me!

Soliloquy of the Stems

In the garden, stems converse,
Debating who's the better curse.
One claims he's the tallest sprout,
While another giggles, "Look, I'm stout!"

They argue back and forth with glee,
About who dreams of being tea.
A radish pipes up, "Not on my watch!"
And then the carrots start to botch!

The daisies roll their eyes in jest,
While the beets just think they're the best.
"Oh, to be rad!" a stem croons sings,
But none can dance like wriggly springs.

And so they prattle 'neath the sun,
In their leafy world of silly fun.
Their verdant chatter fills the air,
As humor grows from roots laid bare.

Whispers from the Woodland

The trees are snickering, what a sight,
As squirrels run around in delight.
"Did you see that nut?" a branch exclaims,
"Looks like dinner's playing games!"

The toadstools giggle at the breeze,
While the acorns float like little peas.
"I'm a hat!" one shouts, "No, I'm a crown!"
As the woods dance up and down.

The owls give knowing looks at night,
While crickets chirp with pure delight.
"Who knew the woods could be so fun?
Let's do this again; where's the sun?"

Leaves rustle softly, a secret tune,
Playing hide and seek with the moon.
"More laughter, please!" the creatures squeak,
In this leafy world, we're all a cheek!

An Arbor's Embrace

In the shade where the branches sway,
The trees all laugh at their own display.
"Look at those birds, they think they're grand!
But who can soar like a leafy hand?"

Underneath, the flowers poke and tease,
"I'm the prettiest, if you please!"
Hollyhocks strut while daisies pout,
And sunflowers shine, all twist and shout.

"Let's throw a party, invite the bees!"
Cried the roses with a giggle and wheeze.
"Your perfume is too strong," a lilac said,
"Let's stick to sweetness instead!"

So the arbors join in mirth and jest,
In nature's waltz, they dance at best.
Together, their laughter breaks the gloom,
In this arboreal, whimsical room.

Blooming Fantasies in Twilight

As the dusk begins to softly glow,
Petals whisper tales from below.
"I dream of candy, sugary sweet,
And giant cookies as the treat!"

"Oh, that's nothing," a poppy tossed,
"I'd rather have a parade, not lost!"
The lilacs buzz with floral hopes,
While violets weave with giddy ropes.

"Twilight giggles," the daisies cheer,
As the stars drop in, ever so near.
"I'll be the moon, shining so bright,
And sprinkle dreams 'til the morning light."

In the twilight, where colors meld,
They dance and twirl, their joy upheld.
A garden of wishes, blooming grand,
In soft embrace, hand in hand.

Enchanted Greenery

In the garden, plants conspire,
Telling jokes that never tire.
Flowers giggle, leaves all sway,
Where the vegetables hold sway.

A cabbage wears a crown of glee,
A carrot thinks it's royalty!
The herbs in whispers, sly and spry,
Debate on who can jump the highest sky.

The sun bursts through in sudden rays,
And all the greens begin their plays.
"Let's have a feast!" the lettuce shouts,
While radishes plot kitchen routes.

On mushroom stools, they sit and trade,
The silliest of garden escapades.
With every breeze, they twist and toss,
In one grand game, none are the boss.

The Dance of Autumn's Veil

Leaves that twirl like ballerinas,
Dressing trees in gold and marinas.
A nutty squirrel dons a hat,
While acorns start a chatter: "That!"

"Shall we put on a grand parade?"
Shouted a twig with a leafy braid.
The breeze agreed, it twirled around,
As laughter echoed from the ground.

A pumpkin joined with great delight,
Told corny jokes that flew like kites.
With every gust, the fun began,
It was the craziest autumn plan!

The trees stretched limbs in zigzag dance,
While critters joined in on a chance.
"Let's spin in circles!" one leaf said,
And soon they soared, all fears were shed.

Secrets Beneath the Shade

Under boughs where shadows play,
Tadpoles whisper tales today.
"Did you see that jumpy frog?"
He sprung from safe, a leafy bog!

A wise old snail in his slow cruise,
Muttered tales of socks and shoes.
"Why wear them? The ground is fine!
Come, let's dance on dandelion!"

The grasshoppers leap with wide-eyed joy,
While ants parade with their tiny toys.
Beneath the shade, a secret fest,
Where every bug feels quite the best.

Moths share stories of moonlight dives,
And everyone laughs at their silly lives.
Underneath the trees, they set the stage,
A comedy of errors, over and sage.

Verdant Reverie

A jungle leaf with a daring grin,
Said, "Let's go out for a spin!"
While vines climbed up, and danced with flair,
It seemed the very sun would stare.

An owl insisted he could sing,
Yet all he chirped was "Cabbage King!"
The parrots squawked, "Well, who's that dude?"
And launched into a berry food feud.

Pine needles sighed in a fit of giggles,
While coming near, a frog just wiggles.
"Who needs the rain, let's have a chat!"
Then under a leaf, he sat with a rat.

From fern to fern, they leaped and spun,
Sprinkling mischief—oh, what fun!
In green attire, they shared their schemes,
Living large in leafy dreams.

Reverberations in the Arboretum

Leaves whisper secrets, so many they share,
They giggle and wiggle, a party up there.
Squirrels dance wildly, on branches they roam,
While owls raise an eyebrow, perched high as their home.

Bouncing around like a well-timed joke,
The petals now chuckle, the thorns have bespoke.
The wind plays a tune, so catchy and bright,
While bunnies beat drums, under soft moonlight.

Branches that bounce back, like rubbery springs,
Wind chimes that chortle and rattle with zing.
Nature's own stand-up, a comedic delight,
As shadows do shuffle, a laugh-out-loud sight.

Whimsical wonders, in colors so grand,
Even the flowers are part of the band.
In every fresh setting, a giggle's in view,
Under the sunbeam, where laughter's anew.

Nature's Palette Unfurled

In the quilt of green, hues frolic with glee,
Yellow suns bother the chill of the tree.
Orange leaves tumble, like clowns in the air,
While violets peek in, with a curious stare.

The red-barked trees pun, with snickers and quips,
As shadows slip softly, with quickened little skips.
Greens join the chorus, in a bright, happy mix,
Their shades play together, like kids with their tricks.

Golden rays giggle, over grass like a joke,
While daisies now tease, with a humorous poke.
Colors collide, in a dance so absurd,
Nature's own artists, with laughter unheard.

As laughter erupts from the wild berry bramble,
The hues of the meadow, a fanciful gamble.
In each painted corner, a smile can be found,
As whimsy and cheer abound all around.

The Curves of the Wild

Nature's got curves, like a dancer on stage,
Wiggly vines tango, uncaged and engaged.
Bended tree trunks, in a comedic pose,
Wind giggles with glee, as it tugs on the bows.

Rolling hills chuckle, they roll with a grin,
While the flowers sport hats, it's the latest trend.
Round mushrooms are stacking, a tower of cheer,
In the curves of the wild, fun is always near.

Curved paths are sneaky, twisty and fun,
They lead us in circles, then back to the sun.
Jumping over roots, like hopping a fence,
The wilderness joins in, with its own sense of sense.

With every small bend, adventure will beckon,
The curves of the wild, are always a reckoning.
So laugh as you wander, and dance all about,
In this wild, silly world, there's no need to pout.

Dappled Thoughts in Nature

Sunlight sprinkles laughter, across the old ground,
As shadows play tag, with a mischievous sound.
A patch of bright daisies, they wink and they sway,
While leaves curtsy kindly, in their own balletic way.

The squirrels are plotting, oh what could it be?
With acorns in hand, they're designed to decree.
Each twist in the path, is a puzzle so grand,
Nature's own humor, all part of the plan.

Under the birches, the toads sing a tune,
Making jokes of their sit, in the light of the moon.
Mushrooms all giggle, in a secretive huddle,
Nature has jokes, if you care to hear muddle.

So wander in dappled, with a smile on your face,
Chase shadows and laughter, at your own easy pace.
For in every rustle, and fluttering flight,
Is a giggle of nature, in pure delight.

www.ingramcontent.com/pod-product-compliance
Lightning Source LLC
Chambersburg PA
CBHW071833160426
43209CB00003B/283